APACHE HELICOPTERS

BY JACK DAVID

BELLWETHER MEDIA · MINNEAPOLIS, MN

Are you ready to take it to the extreme?
Torque books thrust you into the action-packed
world of sports, vehicles, and adventure. These books
may include dirt, smoke, fire, and dangerous stunts.
WARNING: read at your own risk.

Library of Congress Cataloging-in-Publication Data

David, Jack, 1968-
  Apache helicopters / by Jack David.
      p. cm. -- (Torque, military machines)
  Summary: "Explains the technologies and capabilities of the latest generation of Apache helicop-
ters. Intended for grades 3 through 7 "--Provided by publisher.
  Includes bibliographical references and index.
  ISBN-13: 978-1-60014-102-7 (hbk. : alk. paper)
  ISBN-10: 1-60014-102-1 (hbk. : alk. paper)
  1. Apache (Attack helicopter)-- Juvenile literature. I. Title. II. Series.

  UG1232.A88D38 2008
  623.74'63--dc22
                                                                      2007012157

This edition first published in 2008 by Bellwether Media.

The photographs in this book are reproduced through the courtesy of the United States Department of
Defense.

CONTENTS

THE APACHE IN ACTION

It's a time of war in the desert. A group of enemy tanks rolls slowly toward a U.S. Army base. They prepare to fire on the base. U.S. officials at the base order a strike against the tanks. Three AH-64D Apache Longbow helicopters rise into the night.

★ FAST FACT ★

The Apache helicopter has a rotor diameter of 48 feet (14.6 meters).

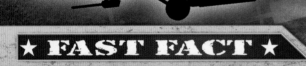

4

6

The pilots fly close to the ground to avoid **radar** detection by the enemy. The Apaches have the enemy tanks within range of their weapons. The commander gives the order: *Fire!*

Missiles strike the tanks. Explosions light up the night. All of the tanks are destroyed within minutes. The Apaches return to the U.S. Army base. They have accomplished their mission.

COMBAT HELICOPTER

The Apache is a valuable tool for the U.S. Army. It is unlike any other helicopter in the world. It is built for fighting and for quick strikes. Its powerful engine makes it fast. Its narrow body and **armor** make it hard to shoot down.

★ FAST FACT ★

The main machine gun is electronically connected to the gunner's helmet—wherever the gunner looks, the gun points!

U.S. ARMY AH-64D
U.S.A SERIAL NO. 98-5100

OOA

Two crew members operate an Apache. The pilot sits in the back seat and flies the helicopter. The **co-pilot gunner (CPG)** sits in the front. The CPG operates the weapons and helps the pilot fly the helicopter.

AH-64D APACHE SPECIFICATIONS:

Primary Function: Attack helicopter

Length: 58 feet (18 meters)

Height: 16 feet (5 meters)

Wingspan: 17 feet (5 meters)

Top Speed: 262 mph (422 km/h)

Range: 300 miles (483 kilometers)

Ceiling: 50,000 feet (15,240 meters)

Weight: 16,600 pounds (7,530 kilograms)

Crew: 2

WEAPONS

The Apache is loaded for battle.
An M230 **machine gun** sits under the nose.
This heavy gun can shoot 600 or more
rounds per minute.

The M230 machine gun

Apache helicopters can take a lot of combat damage and still continue their missions.

Hellfire guided missile

Each launcher holds 19 Hydra rockets.

The Apache can fire missiles capable of destroying armored targets. Its deadliest weapon is the Hellfire guided missile. The missile has a guidance system that locks onto its target. This means the Hellfire can even hit moving targets.

The Apache can also fire 2.75-inch Hydra rockets. The rockets aren't guided like the Hellfire. But they're just as deadly for targets that are standing still.

APACHE MISSIONS

The U.S. Army uses the Apache for a variety of missions. Its primary mission is to carry out surprise attacks. It also guards bases and supports troops on the ground. The U.S. Army first used the AH-64 Apache in 1984. An improved version called the AH-64D Apache Longbow followed in 1998.

★ FAST FACT ★

The Apache can detect and fire on targets day or night.

The Apache's speed and powerful weapons make it the perfect attack helicopter. The crew gets in, destroys their targets, and gets out quickly. The Apache's quick strike capability helps make it the best combat helicopter in the world.

GLOSSARY

armor—protective plating

co-pilot gunner (CPG)—the crew member who operates an Apache helicopter's weapons and helps the pilot fly it

machine gun—an automatic weapon that rapidly fires bullets

missile—an explosive launched at targets on the ground or in the air

mission—a military task

radar—a sensor system that uses radio waves to locate objects in the air

TO LEARN MORE

AT THE LIBRARY
Braulick, Carrie A. *U.S. Army Helicopters*. Mankato, Minn.: Capstone Press, 2006.

Budd, E. S. *Military Helicopters*. Chanhassen, Minn.: Child's World, 2002.

Hansen, Ole Steen. *The AH-64 Apache Helicopter*. Mankato, Minn.: Capstone Press, 2006.

ON THE WEB
Learning more about military machines is as easy as 1, 2, 3.

1. Go to www.factsurfer.com

2. Enter "military machines" into search box.

3. Click the "Surf" button and you will see a list of related web sites.

With factsurfer.com, finding more information is just a click away.

INDEX